Erika D. Newton

FLOETIC ASCENSION
of a
LOTUS

*I'm just a wildflower
Picked from the plains of Sharon,
A lotus blossom from the valley pools*

Song of Songs 2:1 (Msg)

Floetic Ascension of a Lotus

All scripture quotations, unless otherwise indicated, are taken from *The Amplified Bible* (AMP). *The Amplified Bible, Old Testament* Copyright © 1965, 1987 by The Zondervan Corporation. *The Amplified New Testament*, Copyright © 1954, 1958, 1987 by The Lockman Foundation. Used by permission.

Copyright © 2011 by Erika D. Newton

All rights reserved. Except as permitted under the U.S. Copyright Act of 1976, no part of this book may be reproduced, distributed, stored in a database or retrieval system, or transmitted in any form or by any means, electronic, mechanical, photocopy, recording or otherwise, without the prior written permission of the author or publisher.

Published by: Erika D. Newton

Edited by: Erika D. Newton
Interior By: Erika D. Newton

Cover Design & Background Photography by:
Angelia M. Baxter - www.TheKreativStudio.com

Printed in the United States of America
Charleston, SC

ISBN-10: 0-615-49674-1
ISBN-13: 978-0-615-49674-0

Library of Congress Control Number: 2011931626

Erika D. Newton

FLOETIC ASCENSION
of a
LOTUS

Christian Poetry

Prose & Spoken-Word

by

Erika D. Newton

Floetic Ascension of a Lotus

Acknowledgements

First, I acknowledge **Mrs. Marcita Keys-Enis..**
You are the medium God used to usher me into
my divine purpose. When my life shattered, you
were there to help me pick up the pieces. I couldn't
ask for a better friend. I love you Chicka!

**Bishop C. Carl
& First Lady Adrienne Smith**
You said to give you *one year* .. & by committing
to the Word that God would use you to speak..
my life would prosper in every area.
God gave me the idea for this book
less than one-year after you spoke those words

Janeyah, My Princess Booka
You showed me how to receive the
Kingdom of God like a little child

Mimi, Kiki & Trae, My children
You bore with me through darkness,
followed me into the Light.. and forgave me

Toi Nichelle, Author & Poet
You are the spiritually unique soul God used
to inspire me to write this book..
in such a creatively courageous way

Sonjay Odds-Eggleton, Playwright
Diva-Darlin, you showed me what it means to
press through against all odds, into manifested glory

Angelia M. Baxter, Kreativ Designer
You gave extensively of yourself to my dream
of realizing this book.. I am awed, I am humbled & my heart
overflows with sincere appreciation for you. Thank you ☺

Floetic Ascension of a Lotus

Foreword

**Congratulations on your first book.
To God be the glory**

The power of words to transcend, to captivate and to speak to the essence of who you are is woven throughout the pages of this book. This is more than just a book of poetry it is a dialogue from God as He speaks through a vessel who has heard from heaven. Erika's spirit speaks volume as she expresses her thoughts through Poetry, Prose & Spoken Word. A highly recommended book for those who are really in love with words that create, change and illuminate the mind.

**Paulette Harper Johnson,
Best Selling, Award Winning Author of**
'That Was Then, This Is Now' &
'Completely Whole'

Floetic Ascension of a Lotus

Erika D. Newton

Introduction

My gumption to produce this book began with one question...

'What would I try if I knew I could not fail?'

As I pondered... that question began to build on itself.. adding others along the same thought pattern..

If there were no boundaries.. no impossibilities, what would I purpose to do? ..To become? If I knew beyond a shadow of a doubt that it **would manifest**, what dream would I intentionally decide to live out in this earth?

Then another question arose in my mind.. a question the roots of insecurity and shame tried vehemently to deny being asked.. much less answered.

If my past truly did not matter.. where I came from, what I did, what was done to me, who my parents were.. WHO I ONCE WAS... what kind of an impact would I deliberately make on this world... knowing beforehand, that I would absolutely.. be successful?

Suddenly.. from the deepest part of me, the answers came..

I would encourage the soul
of every broken woman..
I would wipe the tears from the heart
of every wounded child..
I would renew the pieces
of every shattered life..
I would be His Light in every dark place..

And how would I accomplish this? Through Christ, & the power of His Spoken Word... and I would begin with this book.

In this book, you will find a few of my life's trials & tribulations poetically woven throughout the pages. My hope for you – the Reader – is that you will be encouraged and inspired to begin to look into the Truth of who and Whose *you really are.*

Floetic Ascension of a Lotus

We have all experienced sorrow, lived through pain, battled with emotions and cried alone in the dark. Some people don't know how to rise up out of that darkness... the darkness of pain, of regret, of shame, of unforgiveness... the darkness of the past. Some perish in that darkness.. never coming into the Light. I believe that this book, for some.. *will reveal* that Light.

For me, this book is the manifested Glory of God.. and it was produced as I trusted Him by faith. 'Faith' is an **action** word. Faith **does**, faith **moves**.. faith is not idle.

For most of my life I have been hurt & I have been knocked down.. HARD! I have been misused, abused, misled & buried under a condemnation that I came to discover DOES NOT **BELONG** TO ME! God Himself helped me to believe.. and by His grace alone, I was able to press this book through!

> *You must simply BELIEVE JESUS! Take a seat at His feet & His grace will empower you to PRESS!*

If you have been hurt.. if you have been knocked down.. HARD, If you have been misused, abused, misled and buried under condemnation.. You too can believe God and press through! Do NOT allow your trials to be wasted by singing those all too familiar 'woe is me' tunes in the dark where NOBODY HEARS YOU!! In Christ, you are a child of the Light. You must simply **BELIEVE JESUS**! Take a seat at His feet & His grace will empower you to PRESS!

Somebody is depending on you to make it.. so that **their** hope to make it can be ignited. The future generation - our children.. are standing behind you waiting on you to knock down doors so that they can pass through *after* you.

Don't allow yourself to be swallowed up in the darkness you may be bathing in by setting your focus on licking yesterdays wounds. Get up and trust God because He is near and is full of love & compassion for you. If you are reading this book, He is near to you NOW!

Slip your hand into the Hand He is extending to you and let Him take you into a Love you have NEVER before experienced.
If you allow Him.. He will lead you into the very purpose He Himself created you specifically **for**. Please understand that you will not walk in your divine purpose without Him.

If you have not yet received Jesus Christ as your Lord and Savior, your time is now. You can refer to the Salvation Prayer in the latter pages of this book to help guide you along.

No matter what your life currently looks like.. no matter what your circumstances are.. and no matter what people have said, are saying, or will ever say about you.. you are valuable beyond measure, precious, cherished and Dearly Loved by the Lord God Almighty. All things are possible for those who believe in God.

Can you overcome?

I am living proof that **YES YOU CAN!**

May this book be a blessing to your life.

Floetic Ascension of a Lotus

Erika D. Newton

Dedication

*To the Trinity..
God The Father,
God The Son &
God The Holy Spirit
You are my everything..
Without You, I am nothing*

*Thank You For Your Life
For It is the Ultimate sacrifice
& Thank you for loving me*

I Love You

"In my fragility..
Death threw me to the ground
And I shattered

Then… Life re-created me

Love obliterated
Every remnant Of brokenness..
Leaving me without even the faintest trace
Of death's residue..

I am His..
I am Restored
I am Complete"

> BLESSED
> (PRAISED AND EXTOLLED
> AND THANKED)
> BE THE LORD,
> THE GOD OF ISRAEL,
> BECAUSE HE HAS COME
> AND BROUGHT
> DELIVERANCE AND
> REDEMPTION
> TO HIS PEOPLE
> **LUKE 1:68 (AMP)**

Table of Contents

Chapter 1
    "Shatter Proof"……………………………..19

Chapter 2
    "Wicked Ways of the Enemy"…...…………..37

Chapter 3
    "The Sound of Conviction"……….………..49

Chapter 4
    "Desires of the Heart"….………..…..……..67

Chapter 5
    "Wayward Butterflies"……..……………...79

Chapter 6
    "Inspirational Discoveries"……..…………….99

Chapter 7
    "Floetic Haiku"……………………….....…109

Chapter 8
    "Let the Children Come"………………..…121

Chapter 9
    "The Truth About Love"…………………..131

Chapter 10
    "Shut Up & Live"………………....………149

Closing Poem
    "Floetic Ascension of a Lotus"………….....162

Receiving Your Salvation…………...…………167

About the Author……………………………...175

*"You cannot thrive in
God's promise of wholeness..
Until you let Him
Have your broken pieces"*

Chapter One
⇛ Shatter Proof ⇚

1.} Still Standing

2.} Hey Little Girl

3.} I Feel Like Crying

4.} Daddy… I Forgive You

5.} In the Midst

6.} People

"Still Standing"

Standing... still standing
Looking back at all the twists & turns,
rubble & stones...
Seeing the blood
on the rocks I left behind
I stand.. still

Looking ahead.. up..
at this road in front of me
I see no thing
No.. **NO** thing
that I cannot overcome..
Because of He Who walks with me

I didn't see Him until I got here
Yet He was with me all along

So much behind..
So many times that I could not walk
Yet, I am here.. Standing
Only now realizing...
It was Jesus Who carried me

Looking ahead..
Knowing He is here
I have already conquered
every mountain, every desert,
every storm & every circumstance

Yes..
Still Standing

Smiling

"Hey... Little Girl"

Little Girl...
I am years ahead of you now...
But.. if I could go back
& give you one piece of wisdom

I would tell you...

That this body you've been assigned to
Is only temporary..

That you must stand..
Through every trial

Even when you
Don't know why you should..
And especially
When you don't know how you can

Hey... Little Girl
I know the **substance** of your tears

I can feel them trickle down your face...
I can taste them on my tongue
As they seep through
The corners of my mouth

I feel you when you wrap your arms
Around myself as your chest heaves
In silent turmoil

You look into the eyes
of people given charge to love you..
Only to see them looking through you..
Loving only themselves

Floetic Ascension of a Lotus

Go ahead and cry little girl...
But Keep standing
Do not trust in what you see
And one day
You will reach up and discover that...

Every single thing intended
For your detriment
God will use for your good

Hey... Little Girl
I know the ***pain*** of your tears

I can feel the blows to my body
When he beats you
Each time the wind is knocked out of you...
I remember you making the choice
To breathe again... ***anyway***

Go ahead and cry little girl...
But keep standing
Do not trust in what you see
And one day you will reach up
And discover that...
Although it appears you are at rock bottom,
The God Who can take you from the pit
to the palace.. loves you deeply
And is ***for*** you

Hey... Little Girl
I know the ***desperation*** of your tears

I can hear your heart strings tearing
Through the tormented voice of my soul
You cling to the false sincerity
Of his smile because
You don't know that you don't know...
What love looks like..

& though your deepest desire
Is to be kept.. to be cherished
You are selfishly rummaged through..
& then like trash.. you are discarded

Go ahead and cry little girl...
But keep standing
Do not trust in what you see
And one day you will reach up
and discover that...

There is an everlasting light in you
Which darkness cannot extinguish

Despite the many evil blows
Your precious spirit sustains..
That light in you... is God ordained
& therefore... will **forever** remain

Hey... Little Girl
I know the *origin* of your tears

You rationalize that maybe...
If your mother hadn't left
Your father would not have
Repetitiously violated you

I can see the ground
As your eyes are cast downward
Under the heaviness of a shame
Which does not belong to you

You are filled to overflowing
With low self-esteem
Desperately wishing yourself dead...
Hating to breathe... day - after day -
After day... after day...

Floetic Ascension of a Lotus

Hey... Little Girl..
I know what your **heart** looks like
Behind that stolen smile

It's broken down in pieces
Struggling with each pump...
& leaking blood with every beat

Go ahead and cry little girl...
But keep standing
Do not trust in what you see
And one day you will reach up
& you will discover that...

He fixed you...

When you were shredded on the inside
From being torn down on the outside.

You will look into the mirror of His Grace
& you will see me
Staring back at you

Then you will know..
That He has given you **ALL** of His Beauty
In exchange for **ALL** of your ashes

A man of God once said to me...
'The deeper the hurt,
The bigger your destiny'

And Little Girl...

It was apparently determined
Before the foundation of the earth
That your destiny...

Is of **monumental** magnitude

Erika D. Newton

Little Girl...
I am years ahead of you now...
But.. if I could go back
& give you one piece of wisdom

I would tell you...

That this body you've been assigned to
Is only temporary..

That you must stand..
Through every trial

Even when you
Don't know why you should..
And especially
When you don't know how you can

Because you are on assignment
& the plight of darkness
Is to blind you to your Light
& annihilate you

So if you must..
Sway with the tempest...
But do not fall
Reach up..

and **LOVE *WILL*** steady you

HE PROMISED!

"I Feel Like Crying"

Fighting back the tears is
Becoming more difficult with each blink
I hate the devil.. he is such a liar
I feel like crying.. so I think I will

Silently.. my tears begin to fall
My heart is sore from stinging words
Words that came out of the heart
Through the mouth
Of someone who truly does love me..

Someone who loves the Lord deeply
Yet they were words I did not deserve
And O Lord.. do those words hurt

'Chin up' my spirit commands
But against my will, tears begin to flow

My breathing becomes deeper
As I try to fight off the intensity of it
My eyes are red now.. bloodshot

My body..
As my chest heaves against my will..
Is attempting to add sound to my tears
But my precious child
Lies asleep beside me

I could go into the bathroom..
But there is a mirror there

The sight of my own tormented eyes
staring hopelessly back at me
Would surely
induce a flood of tears..

They would stream down my face
at an uncontrollable pace

I could go into the closet..
But the darkness inside would mock me..
The suffocating atmosphere would
Cause the deep, insuppressible sound
Of my cries to reverberate off of the walls

Deep cries given to desperation
Cause nerve wrenching distortion
As facial muscles twist in peculiar form

My child would hear & be despaired
If she opened the door
To find her mommy in such a state

I could go outside..
And hide silently among the passers by
Denying my soul the release
It so urgently demands

But then the anguish..
Throbbing incessantly in my bones
Would remain pent up..
To fester and build.. only to later explode
Undoubtedly at some **other** inopportune time

Or worse.. my cries could implode.
.
Leaving me far less than empty
Filled with regret, shame & bitterness..
Enveloped by a deep absolute sense of..

Nothingness

I could run a bath..

Floetic Ascension of a Lotus

Then, no one would hear my weeping..

For the sound of my cries
Would be lost in the roar of the water
As it fills the tub...

& I could lock the door
So no one but God will see

And if my weeping becomes sobbing..

I would twist each faucet handle
To its utmost extreme..
Causing the sound of the water to
Escalate from a roar..
To a continuous explosion
As it bursts forth with thunderous force

And if my sobbing becomes wailing...

I would turn the water off..
Get into the tub.. and
Inhale deeply before I..

Sink myself down
To wail.. as I exhale..
Underwater

Fighting back those tears
Became more difficult with each blink
I hate the devil.. he is such a liar
I felt like crying..

and I'm glad I did

"Daddy, I Forgive You"

Daddy... I forgive you

I forgive you for dying
Before I could muster up
The courage to confront you
Not for your sake.. but for my own
& for my freedom...

**I forgive you
For the damage God has undone**

I forgive you for being weak,
Foolish, evil and perverted
For looking upon me in a way
No father should ever
Look upon his own

For stealing the sincerity of my smile
For tainting the heart of my personality..
& for challenging my will to live

Daddy.. I forgive you

**I forgive you
For stealing my innocence**
Using the hand God gave you...
The same hand..
That held mine so many times

The same hand..
God gave you to protect
& cherish me

I forgive you

Floetic Ascension of a Lotus

For bringing into manifestation
Your wicked thoughts

For assuming
That a child could feign sleep
Through such excruciating..
Mind altering pain

I was horrified..

Through my shallow breathing..
Through my feeble attempt to
lie motionless... I was hiding

So very terrified
That you would know I was awake
By my slight but uncontrollable shaking..
Caused by the extreme intensity of a pain...
That my mind before that..
Was incapable of imagining..

Daddy... I forgive you

I forgive you for forcing me to suffer
Through the agonizing torture of you
Irrefutably evident in..
The tears involuntarily released..
Flowing silent & hot
Down the sides of my face
Forever staining my cheeks..
Flooding my ears before falling to my pillow..
I wished myself dead

I forgive you for my agony
Burning in the precious blood
Brought forth by your hand..

I forgive you for not looking ahead

At the dire consequences
Your self-seeking pleasure would have
Upon my mind, will and emotions

I forgive you

For being blindly consumed
By the superficiality of your lust

I forgive you

For the years you've invested in..
Turning off the light in my 9 year old mind
Warping the love in my 10 year old heart
& so selfishly polluting my 11 year old soul

I forgive you

For stripping my daddy away from me..
I so admired him

I was proud of my daddy
Oh how I loved him so..
With all of my 8 year old heart
To me.. he was stronger..
& far better.. than even Superman
I was wrong.. so very wrong

Daddy... I forgive you

I forgive you for dying
Before I could muster up
The courage to confront you
Not for your sake.. but for my own
& for my freedom...

**I forgive you
For the damage God has undone**

Floetic Ascension of a Lotus

"In the Midst"

In the midst of my body suffering
through wounds of wickedness
my spirit evolved..
and emerged victoriously..
without blemish

Every blow inflicted upon my body..
polished a dull, tarnished area
of my spirit

until Hell became blinded
by my Gleam

Every heart string
brutally ripped from my chest
caused a broken piece of my spirit
to be re-attached..
Seamlessly

In the midst of death
trying desperately to claim my soul..
my spirit awakened to a New Birth..
a humble swelling of Mighty Power

While my body was struck dumb
with a peculiar feeling that
sunk deeper than the superficiality
of excruciating pain..
my spirit floated effortlessly
on the cottony heights of
revelatory existence

Erika D. Newton

In the midst of emerging womanhood
blood began to flow
which, through trial & tribulation..
would be trampled heartlessly underfoot..

Until the Living Water became the flow..
replacing the blood lost..

which.. I later discovered..
was intentionally stolen from me
with my eyes open wide shut

The dirt that once clogged every pore
& identified every orifice
of the lie that proclaimed to be my life..
has become a spotless declaration..

It is my banner held high..
reaching far above the floors of heaven..
founded on the mercy seat
in the very Throne Room of God

This banner testifies
by the manifested beauty inside of me..

A Holy beauty..
which has permanently replaced
the ashes of a life...

that can no longer touch me

Yes!

Floetic Ascension of a Lotus

In the midst of a corrupted soul
flourishing in immaturity..
Divinity commanded my true essence
to overcome..
even as a spiritual embryo

The devil had me
right where God wanted me
Though I assisted
in its sinister effort to do so
death wasn't strong enough
to take my life

For every piece
torn from my mind, will & emotions..

A peace was given to replace it
gracefully.. repetitiously until..
Wholeness revealed Himself
in my entirety

In the midst of my body suffering
through wounds of wickedness
my spirit evolved..
and emerged victoriously..
without blemish

Every blow inflicted upon my body..
polished a dull, tarnished area
of my spirit

until Hell became blinded
by my Gleam

Erika D. Newton

"People"

People...

They smile in your face
Unaware they are being betrayed
By the darkness in their eyes

While your back is turned,
Persecution flows from their perverse lips
Into the thirsty ears of others

I sometimes wonder...

Do they stand in the mirror
Practicing their glued-on smiles?

People...

Isn't it interesting how they...
Pat you on the back and exclaim

'Good Job!'

Only to wait impatiently for your exit..
After which, they Initiate
'Project Defamation'

People...

Back-biting slanderers roam the earth..
Disguised as Angels of Light..

And some have no idea
That they themselves are these very

People

The lost lead the lost
Like the blind read the map..
Without a vision

Chapter Two

≫ Wicked Ways of the Enemy ≪

1.} The World

2.} Crevices

3.} Superficial Prosperity of the Wicked

4.} Plea of a Rejected Minor

5.} Prayer Against the Enemy

6.} Man's Words

7.} Crop Failure

"The World"

The world will attempt to lasso you *in*
for the soul purpose of
wrapping you around its seductive finger..
representative of a past no longer yours

The world cannot comprehend
that your slate has been wiped clean
Cannot grasp the concept
that you have been redeemed

The hands of the world
operate in chaos...
with much skill & proud delight

The feet of the world
dance precariously... in darkness
every premeditated step
foolishly mocking Light itself

The head of the world
tilts backwards on its self-righteous neck
of twisted enjoyment

Its faith reversed & consumed...

tainted by the tangible mirage of
delusional.. deceivingly beautiful..
superficialities

The eyes of the world
are incapable of tolerating illumination
its lids are shut tight
it is fooled.. and unfortunately subdued
by the darkness it sees..
yet does not discern

Erika D. Newton

"Crevices"

Crevices

he creeps through
believing he goes unnoticed

He fights the truth..

that darkness cannot exist
where Light reigns

&

because the Light
possesses an intelligence
he can never have..

his shadows can no longer hide

Yet... & Still...

To his preordained ruin
He craftily surrounds himself
In the futility of false light
to lie in wait ...

Only to be divinely & inevitably

Exposed

"Superficial Prosperity of the Wicked"

Superficial prosperity of the wicked
slowly bring them
to their inevitable demise

In lieu of their unanticipated doom...
they relax as they
covet..
as they lie..
as they defile

Worshipping illusionary paradise
royally uncovered
in terrestrial garb..

Smiling.. fleshly fixated
outwardly pleased..
as darkness expertly infiltrates the core

They are blindly drenched with evil
DRIPPING...
with the blood of the world

Erika D. Newton

"Plea of a Rejected Minor"

Just.. smile at me man...
I'll be whateva you want me to be
I know you don't love me.. & that's ok
But.. if you say you do, I'll give you all of me
& I'll smile right back at you

Just.. smile at me man
Been rejected all my life
Used, abused, broken, tattered & torn
I wished on many a tear..
That I was neva eva born

Just.. smile at me man
Let me be what love means to you
I just need you to pretend for a while.. cuz
Sweet lies dripping from your lips...
Out-weigh the bitter torture of me against me

Just.. smile at me man
Because I'm all alone inside myself
Too much blood left on issues unresolved
My wish.. which will inevitably become my regret
Is that I were someone other
Than the tormented soul in the mirror

Just.. smile at me man
& say you love me..
But look away when you do.. &

Forget about the damaged little girl
With the intensely defeated eyes
Starin back at you

Just.. smile at me man..

Please?

Floetic Ascension of a Lotus

"Prayer Against the Enemy"

Father God..
In the Name of Jesus I pray

Expose those who are
speaking lies over me
Father, expose those who have
wickedness in their hearts concerning me

Let not your chosen people
of the house you sent me to
be moved by words of deceit
For discord is being sown..
which is an abomination to You O Lord

Let not the leaders
you have called me to submit to
fall victim to concocted woes
further poisoned by
premeditated tears of manipulation,
selfishness, envy, unforgiveness & hate

Let not your set man
and those that represent his beard
become a respecter of persons Lord God..
looking upon me as suspect, as unrighteous
or as an untrue conversion..

Let them not be duped into seeing me
through eyes of pity & disdain

I beseech You..
Search my heart Father.. my inmost parts
Expose satan everywhere he is O God..
Your daughter in Christ, my Savior
Amen

Erika D. Newton

"Man's Words"

Just because man declared it
Does not make it so
Be weary when words are drenched in honey
With no hint of salt in their flow

Do not receive as truth
All the things you see, hear or read
For everything revealed to your senses
Is not to be believed

Jumping to conclusions
Only leads to confusion
Decisions made based on such
Are manifested delusion

Words spoken in fallacy
Whether intentional or not
Lack the Spirit of Truth
& ironically.. by the most educated scholar
might not be caught

Pray that your hearing be anointed
That you may listen among the deep
Only with divine comprehension
Will you perceive what & which Spirits speak

Words penetrate deeper
Than most could imagine
Our very surroundings are tangible evidence
Of our faith-filled thoughts spoken-out

Words promote love, fear, courage & hate
They advocate freedom, bondage, war & peace
They speak poverty, wealth, life & death..
They operate in truth, lies, fiction & fact

Floetic Ascension of a Lotus

Every word **believed**.. is a word **received**
& thereby endorses & authorizes
Its visible manifestation

Words can draw blood..
& leave you dying by the wayside
Words like 'I don't believe in Jesus Christ' or
'There's no such thing as eternal life'

Words can penetrate through the bone
& spill your marrow on erroneous ground
Words like 'Nobody will ever love you' or
'You'll always be broke, gullible & worthless'

Words can change minds for better or worse
Words like 'Come here honey,
Daddy wants to pull up your pretty lil dress' or
'It's my fault that he beats me.. but he loves me'

Words can edify, uplift & ignite greatness
Empowering one to overcome
Words like 'You've got what it takes to prosper' or
"God made you on purpose &
His hands are only capable of beauty'

Words can spark a revolution, revival or revolt
Words like 'I'm not giving up my seat' or
'I have a dream today' or
'I have come, that you might have Life
& have it more abundantly'

The prowess of a demagogue
is measured by the electrifying charm
of his spoken-word.. but Christ.. **IS** the Word

Because man declared it - does not make it so
Be weary when words are drenched in honey
With no hint of salt in their flow

"Crop Failure"

Every time I choose to sleep
when my Father commands me to rise..
my disobedience permits the evil one
to sit upon my eyes

When I finally awake..
I am reminded
of the choice I made
to be spiritually blinded

I stare at the ceiling..
unwilling to pull myself up
To describe it literally.. it is as if I am stuck
Stuck under the heavy pressure
of a condemnation
that is not supposed to exist for me

I have grieved the Holy Spirit..
& I don't know how to apologize.
My spirit inside is reaching up
and digging down all at the same time

My face is expressionless
Though in silence..
my soul cries out in shrieks
Lord.. I am so sorry I hurt You..
and It burns so deep to know that I chose to

My duty is to surrender to my spirit..
not to yield to my flesh
Oh God.. what have I done?

Floetic Ascension of a Lotus

I have detached myself.. I have fallen

The enemy is trying to convince me
That I am no longer blessed

LORD... I repent.
Forgive me Lord..
Search my heart O God
and extract all of that which is not of You
Reveal it to me Lord..
and lead me in Your way everlasting.

I RECEIVE YOUR FORGIVENESS

))))) THE DEVIL IS A **LIAR** !! (((((

Attention satan and
every one of your demonic cohorts
after I wrote the first half of this..
I went to church & heard the Truth
See.. I was reminded that
I'VE GOT MAIL

God placed my word
In the mouth of the Chosen Man
& He confirmed
what my spirit was trying to remind me of...

I've got mail!!
& devil you're angry
because you can't return it to my Sender!

So go ahead...

throw your lil fiery dart tantrums
For in Christ.. I will SURELY outlast it

I am the righteousness of God in Christ
and to boldly approach the throne is my
BLOOD BOUGHT RIGHT

I cried out to the Lord
in TRUE repentance.. and
Because I've had a change of heart,
a change of mind
and a change of direction,
He was just to forgive me

He has promised me victory over you
as long as I choose to dwell in Him
And as I submit myself to Him
He empowers me to resist you
& you must flee

So in the Name of JESUS
I DECLARE **CROP FAILURE**
On every thought I gave credence to
& every word I gave voice to
that contradicts the Word of God for my life

Now devil

That eliminates what I spoke in your favor..
& it eternally deletes
What you *thought* you heard

THANK YOU FATHER IN **JESUS'** NAME

Floetic Ascension of a Lotus

The longer you wait to speak..
The longer you remain ineffective.

Unleash the articulated wisdom of God...
Unlock your courage
to speak when Spoken through

Chapter Three
⇶ The Sound of Conviction ⇷

1.} Anger Is Appropriate

2.} That's the Atmosphere

3.} What Is It About Me

4.} Mediocrity

5.} The Word 'Love'

6.) Don't Let Go

"Anger Is Appropriate"

I knew not t'was noble to be angry
For righteousness' sake

Righteous indignation
Towards a dark situation
Ignited a fiery sensation
In the pit of my belly

Blood boiling hot
My emotions pushed forth
Like a tidal wave
In a raging attempt to
Burst through my veins

Teeth clenched.. eyes narrow
My minds eye focused
Straight as an arrow

Meticulously deliberating
Purposefully premeditating
On this frustrating thing which
Meant to be debilitating
BUT...

It failed horribly in its attempt

))))) **HALLELUJAH!!!** (((((

Avoiding spiritual confiscation
& defamation by retaliation
I stripped the power from my flesh..

Humbly surrendering to my spirit

After repentance came revelation..

Meekness is NOT weakness

Anger is appropriate...
When harnessed appropriate-*ly*

Though it is not always okay
to speak my mind

It is just fine
To let my spirit reign..

Vocally

Floetic Ascension of a Lotus

"That's the Atmosphere"

Just add a few **'Whoop Whoops!'**
over a real tight beat
and that's the atmosphere
in which they'll listen to God speak

He knows just how to reach you
no matter where you are
In a house, under the freeway,
holding on to a drink at the bar
Or leaning back,
hiding underneath your hoodie
in the car

This goes out
to all of you religious pretenders
The ones who look away..
who won't stop to pray for the sinners

You won't look past yourselves long enough
to see the pain of those who hurt
because you're too content
gossiping about the girl in the 3rd pew
wearing the short skirt

God is **BIGGER**
than the religious box you try to put Him in

He created diversity.. and in His personality,
He fit every one of His children in

Yet..

most of you would never step foot
in the dirt that He found me in

Erika D. Newton

because you can't see past the false light
you're standing so haughtily in

I represent the same God you claim to
& I'm covered by the Same Blood
Saved, sanctified & Holy Ghost filled
I'm holy and I'm consecrated
drenched in God's Love

Some of you say..
I ain't Christ-like cuz I'm wearin jeans
Cuz I ain't rockin {yet}
with some of them finer things

Some of you even think that God don't rap..
it's only Holy if it's sing-songy
You turn your perfect little nose up
at the lyrical swag I bring

But He said I would be persecuted..
that my faith would be tested
See.. He already warned me.

He let me know from the gate
that I would be messed with
And I was instructed to remain in Him..
to walk after the Spirit

So, I stay in His presence..
and I know His voice when I hear it
Every other voice is foreign..
so I don't go near it

You judge me by my clothes..
telling me I need to change up

But my jeans pressed up –
crease is perfectly centered and starched up

Floetic Ascension of a Lotus

While your suit is more wrinkled
than the nose you're turning up
Black shoes showing grey
where the tips are all scuffed up

And I ain't clownin.. I'm just sayin
stop trippin on the **wrong *stuff***

I was sent here to tell you
not to judge a book by its cover
That's the way of the world..
God's way is to love one another

Judge me by my fruit
Not by the color or condition of my
3-piece, 2-piece, or no piece suit

And don't let anybody tell you
God don't go to the hood
My bible says God is Omni-present..
and in ALL ways.. Good

When Jesus died.. He went to hell..
so I wouldn't have to go
That alone tells me..
there is no place the Livin God won't go

I said..

When Jesus died.. He went to hell..
so I wouldn't have to go
That alone tells me..
there is no place the Livin God won't go

He just added a few **'Whoop Whoops!'**
over a real tight beat
And that's the atmosphere
in which I heard God speak

"What Is It About Me"

What is it about me
that disturbs you so deeply?

Are you upset that my identity
was revealed to you in the midst
of you throwing your
self-righteous daggers at me?

Is it because you want so desperately
to be the Love that I am?

Does my confidence cause
your blood to boil?

Why do you persecute me?
Is it the truth in my authoritative tone
when I speak of the Life
that you only pretend to live?

Are you afraid of being uncovered?

Why do you exert your energy
so **passionately**
in trying to shut my mouth?

Do you not know who you are?
Or is it that you are utterly petrified
of who you are **not**?

Why did you think your words
would hurt me?

Did you honestly believe..
that your attempt to draw blood
through your articulate accusations...

Floetic Ascension of a Lotus

would cause me to bow.. **defeatedly**?

You thought I would cower
in some dark corner didn't you?

Why do you tremble so?
Is it because I choose to stand
behind my Father and face you?

Or is it simply because...

you find it difficult to maintain stability
on your precarious foundation of straw?

Why do you attempt
to run & hide behind your words
when transparency
is the only inevitable result?

How is it that you proclaim
to be in love with my Father
when you allow the words of the enemy
to flow so loosely.. so impulsively..
from your bitterly enraged lips?

Where in the **Word**
does it support your insulting me?

Did you forget
that when you leave the sanctuary..
you remain the church?

Do you not know
that when you curse me...
you do it in futility?

Why are you so visibly disgusted & confused
by the genuine sincerity of my smile?

Do you think...
that you are bigger than me?
Better than me? Smarter than me?

You think
that you are better off than me
don't you?

Is that why you're so
condescending towards me?

You think...
that I walk in my own power don't you?
You have no idea...
Who walks before me... do you?

Do you find it frustrating
being blinded by the light infiltrating me?
What is it like walking in darkness...
pretending to see?

Why do you burn
with such fierce anger towards me?

What is it about me
that disturbs you so deeply?

Are you upset that my identity
was revealed to you in the midst
of you throwing your
self-righteous daggers at me?

Is it because you want so desperately
to be the Love that I am?

"Mediocrity"

Why?

Is human mediocrity
So prevalent... & rampant
Among those who
Call themselves Christians?

Mediocrity does not exist
Around the Throne...

Where Are You?

Voluntary spiritual starvation
Brings death upon a worldly obese nation
Unsound infrastructure..
Like bones without marrow
Surround a feeble, malnourished core
Sucked dry by the embedded words
Of the lifeless

Contaminated faith is
The darkness.. the mockery
That cloaks the path of many
who have Forgotten their righteousness

Their faces.. set like flint
Towards Spiritual stagnation

They are aware... but oblivious
Of the Lord our God

RISE in remembrance of Divine implantation
The blood that covers you
Commands your recollection of this truth..

He Who is in you is **Greater**
Than he who is in the world.

Meditation brings about revelation
of Heavenly identification
Resulting in victorious manifestation
Of , in, through & for **You!...**
His glorious New Creation

But before obedience.. **Submission** is key.
For, how can we begin to be obedient
without first **submitting**
To the Father we were created to obey?

Submit to His proven Love for you
Submit to His desire to prosper you
In every area of your life
Stop trying to save yourself..
You will fail.. His Will cannot

Wisdom & direction..
In their proper form..
Can only be given by God.. &

Can only be obtained.. through Christ

The beauty is in the allegiance
& Determination of the spirit

**Hell hath no fury
Like a true Christian informed**

True Christianity informed
Is omnipotent power unleashed
Satan has no authority
Where the Blood infiltrates

Thus, in the intensity of hells fury..
For the soul purpose of destroying the mind..
Fiery darts are strategically
Aimed & launched... but

Only to be faithfully decreed futile..
Cut short.. rejected..
By the engraved Truth that..

NO WEAPON FORMED AGAINST ME
WILL **EVER** PROSPER
For 'It is finished' said the Lord!

Therefore, I Cannot be overcome
By the devil or any demon in hell

Because I've discovered that..
I am on the offense
And... I've Got Mail..

Oh yeah.. you owe me satan
And I've come to collect.. &
I did not come to wager
So stick your pitchfork up your bet

The Blood.. MINE

The fruit of the Spirit.. MINE
Prosperity.. MINE
Every Covenant right.. MINE
The childhood you stole.. MINE
The Power to do all things
through Christ Who strengthens me.. MINE

The Authority to trample you.. MINE

Eternally.. MINE

Defeat.. YOURS
Eternally.. YOURS

With Power such as this
Bestowed upon the true body of Christ..
I wonder..

Why?

Is human mediocrity
So prevalent... & rampant
Among those who
Call themselves Christians?

Mediocrity does not exist
Around the Throne...

Where Are You?

"The Word 'Love' "

Love..
Love is sent from above
Straight from He Who *is* Love
Pure as the white
God painted on the dove

Everybody needs it..
every man, woman, boy & girl
Some may deny it..
tis the way of a hard hearted world

For the word 'love'..
many have a warped definition
The evidence is discovered
in the way that they are livin

The word 'love' means nothing
without the application
But most don't understand,
even those ruling the nation,
That the abuse of Love.. simply put,
is unholy infiltration

See.. growin up, they had it all bad
So now.. their heart is on vacation
Visible absentees steering blindly
through loveless situations

Deceived in childhood
by false confessions of love
resulted in confused alienation

Now they dish it how they got it..
soul contamination
And on the deepest level..

it's spiritual misrepresentation
a faith violation

Mental, physical, sexual abuse

Spiritual too..
if you don't know how & what
to bind and loose

Now we're getting down to the nerve,
where it really hurts
People are scared to talk
about the abuse getting served
on a platter in the church

Hidden in the smiles & claps
of the congregation
Battered wives hiding black eyes
under Maybeline & Mac

and

That they were able to hold on
one more day without killin him..
is why they're praisin

Hot tears streaming down their faces
mistaken for elation.. Yet

They stay religiously planted in abuse..
Believing God ordained their
imagined state of 'holy degradation'

Children in the church
with twisted imaginations
Because they're too afraid
to tell someone about the molestation

Floetic Ascension of a Lotus

The ones that do tell
are not believed

They're put to shame
when their violator claims defamation

So they close their little eyes & try to hold on
for whatever the duration
Looking forward to their adulthood..

Thinking they'll be safe then..
Childhood stolen..
Never to be lived again

Some choose to let go before
God can reach them
The ones that hold on
become vessels He uses to teach them

Though abuse may stain your past..
God takes those scars and deletes them
Those who believe Him..
He sanctifies, consecrates
& eternally redeems them

The Love that is God eradicates
Strips bare, makes new &
Divinely propagates...

Exposes lies by the word True Love dictates
The power of His Light
Allowing darkness no hiding place
Because real Love..

Is sent from above
Straight from He Who **is** Love
Pure as the white
God painted on the dove

Erika D. Newton

"Don't Let Go"

No matter what you're going through
or what circumstances do to you...
call His Name.. & don't let go

I know it gets hard sometimes..
watching the wicked scheme & prosper
while you struggle to avoid the welfare line...
call His Name.. & don't let go

When you feel your grip slippin
because the people who say they love you
only judge you & refuse to listen...
though your knuckles turn white
hold on tight...
call His Name.. & don't let go

Because when you call His Name
He comes running to you and...

He sees what you're going through...
because everywhere you are, He goes
He knows it gets hard sometimes...
because He's with you, softening the blows
He'll hold you up when your grip slips...
because your white knuckles.. He knows

You will overcome.. if

No matter what you're going through
or what circumstances do to you...
you call His Name.. &

DON'T LET GO

When the tempter comes,
It is a set-up for failure..
Flee
When the test comes,
It is a set-up for promotion..
Press

❧{ **Minister Rene Hanible** }☙

Chapter Four
⇒ **Desires of the Heart** ⇐

1.} I Want To See You Deep

2.} Love… Touch

3.} Just Repetition

4.} Rivers Run Deep

5.} Not Yet Spoken

"I Want To See You Deep"

I pray..
That your spirit be exposed to mine

If you are not already Gods man..
Then, with my soul, you will not dine
For it is not possible
that you should be mine

I want to see past your eyes..
Past your heart

&..

Far past the mere depth of your soul

Your spirit is
Who, what, where and how..
You are

You could never know you
Like your spirit knows you

I want to see you.. deep

So deep...

That only God
can see you deeper

"Love... Touch"

Love... touch me
Leave my dreams and manifest

I thirst for the truth of your kiss..
The warmth of your caress...
The tender sincerity of your voice
conveying how much I mean to you

You are genuine..

Never in my natural life...
Have I had the pleasure of...

Being the center of your attention..
of being the focus of your affection

My heart cries out for you..
Do you exist in the earth?
Will I ever know you?
Do you look for me?

Why is it that...
I can hear you calling out to me?

I long for the heartfelt passion
evident in your embrace.

The warmth of your breath as you
whisper the truth of your love in my ear
stains my heart & makes heavy my tears...

Floetic Ascension of a Lotus

They run down my cheeks like bricks of lead
when I allow the thought
that you may never find me...
to penetrate

Where are you?

I miss you with an ache
deeper than human language
can explain.

Tell me how that can be possible
when I have never known you???

My marrow cries out 'Whose rib am I?'

For you.. I will not search
I cannot allow history to repeat itself.
Instead.. I will wait for you
to find me.. to see me.. to claim me

Then and only then
will my love touch you
I will leave your dreams and manifest

Your thirst will be quenched
by the truth of my kiss..
by the warmth of my caress
& by the tender sincerity of my voice
conveying how much you mean to me

I am genuine

Erika D. Newton

"Just Repetition?"

Is it all just repetition?

Because if that's all it is.. I want no part
I'd rather leave wrong choices chosen not
So as not to contribute yet again..
to my own broken heart

Same dance.. different partner
That is all it seems to be
The ups cannot be uniquely distinguished
the downs are all too familiar

When they love you..
They buy you flowers..
Take you out for a good time.. and
they may even hold your hand

But once familiarity sets in..
The phone stops ringing.. &
They blindly walk upon 'greener grass'
too selfish to water their own..

Is lovemaking ever truly made in love?
Or is it simply intercourse...
Intertwined with false intentions and
lust-filled lies sweetly spoken?

They smile with their eyes..
They caress you with carefully engineered
sensitivity & understanding,

Floetic Ascension of a Lotus

They form the words 'I do'
as they vow to honor and keep you

Only to take your heart
into the palms of their tainted hands
to deceitfully.. carelessly.. leave it to die
between the lust filled thighs
of immorality

It is not my desire
to dance the same dance..
Divinity must intercede
I seek, wait & long for..

Love.. in it's purest form

To be one...
with the man God has set apart for me..
is.. and can only be.. Love

To be held simply
because his heart commands
his arms to enfold me
Is a desire that floods
through the depths of my soul

The wife of a God sent man.. Wow!
As simple as that thought seems..

It cuts infinitely deeper
than human words could ever
develop the ability to explain

Erika D. Newton

Oh how my heart rejoices
at the mere thought of walking hand in hand..
Creating memories in places foreign to the trails
he's blazed with women before me

I imagine relaxing in the comfort
& strength of his arms.. listening for hours..
All the while knowing
that he has never spoken in such love
to anyone else but God

If only it could be different this time..
I need it to be the truth..
of Divine substance.

For him to desire the same quality
At an even deeper level than I do..
Would be sublime.. blissful even

I will wait forever.. because…

I'd rather be left alone if..
I cannot have deep, genuine,
heaven sent Love

Is it all just repetition?

Because if that's all it is.. I want no part
I'd rather leave wrong choices chosen not
So as not to contribute yet again..

to my own broken heart

Floetic Ascension of a Lotus

"Rivers Run Deep"

Preliminary electricity inevitable..
clearly undeniable.. but
my rivers run deep

Is the electric current
flowing through your veins
deposited from on High?
Or am I simply the battery
that powers you for the moment?

We stand... close
Your arms about my waist
in precisely the right place
Initial eye contact
ignites curious flames...

But the depth of true love..
Does not exist in superficiality,
Therefore.. deeper.. we must go

Eye contact unbroken intensifies
The fiery penetration of our stares
Unmasking vulnerabilities..
Exposing insecurities

Mutual attraction, although apparent..
Is now profound in its refreshed definition

Yet.. deeper still we must go

Breathing becomes impassioned...
& peculiarly rapid
As eye contact remains unbroken

Suddenly, we are mutually hesitant

Confined within the heat
of words unspoken

This is the infernal abyss
which swallows many...
Too many
But my rivers run deep

So I choke those unspoken words..
leaving them to drown..
in waters of life.. and purity

I am introduced to the strength of your arms
as you boldly pull me closer
security breach physically impossible
Eye contact holding strong

Still.. deeper we must go

Hovering above the depths of our
spiritual awareness
We want to... we desire to...

Impossible to please our heavenly Father
if we do..

We obediently choose not to..
praying this to be the Love
we both waited so long..
& hoped so hard for

Yes.. deeper still.. we must go

If in your still depths I stand.. and
Look into your eyes long enough..
deep enough.. to see beyond
the predictable membrane
of fleshly desire

Will I see Christ?

If in my still depths you stand.. and
Look into my eyes long enough..
deep enough.. to see beyond
the volatile membrane
of invulnerability..

when you see Christ..
will you stand.. still?

After a thousand kisses
What will the beat of your heart
say about me?

After familiarity of you permeates me..
will I find someone else.. someone dark..
lurking beneath your skin?

Will the unspoken words of
steady.. intense.. eye contact
remain as volcanic as that initial stare..
before the eruption of that first kiss?

If we uncover ourselves
before we've looked into each other
long enough.. deep enough..

We will never know

Eye contact must remain
Unbroken.. focused.. & undefiled

Our rivers must.. run deep

Erika D. Newton

"Not Yet Spoken"

The wounds of my voice

Seep from the pain of words

Not yet spoken

Teetering on the edge of

the lower lip of hope...

Omission maintains its balance

My words take the fighter's stance

Against the breath of dreams

Not yet broken

'Speak when Spoken through'

My spirit silently commands

'For it is the residue...

Trying desperately

To reclaim the inner man'

*You must first have the capacity
to discern the distraction…
Before you can operate
in the ability to look beyond it*

Chapter Five

⫷ **Wayward Butterflies** ⫸

1.} He Is

2:} Someone

3.} Don't Wanna

4.) You

5.} In My Belly

6.} Lord, If You Sent Him

7.} On Death's Bed

"He Is"

He is...

A soft spirit...

His stare is soft
His touch is soft
His intentions are soft

Softly dancing
upon the edge of my curiosity

He is...

A sweet spirit...

His heart is sweet
His conversation is sweet
His smile is sweet

Sweetly courting
the essence of my being

He is...

A gentle spirit...

His walk is gentle
His hugs are gentle
His lead is gentle

Gently summoning my thoughts
to wrap around the possibility of him

Erika D. Newton

"Someone"

I wonder if the thought of me
has ever crossed his heart
Has he ever closed his eyes
& chased me along the ocean shore?

Has he ever..
just before drifting off to sleep...
turned the corners of his mouth up
at the memory of my smile?

I wonder if he knows that I pray for him..
That I am truly standing in the gap for him..
That I adore the sound of his laugh...
I wonder if this is simply the flaw
of a presumptuous imagination..

To picture someone fitting the profile of
'The Ideal Mate'.. In love with you...
sharing their life with you

To imagine.. & even dream of
what a disagreement would be like..
What it would feel like to be
held securely in the arms of this..

someone

When I close my eyes..
I slip my hand into his
as he leads me to the dance floor..

Floetic Ascension of a Lotus

I can feel his hands
gently resting at the small of my back..
I am caressing the soft curls of his hair
With my arms about his neck

And though there are
many other couples dancing..
flirting, laughing & loving
we are so deep in love.. that
we only see each other

Then I open my eyes & realize
That.. maybe..

He doesn't think about me at all...
Maybe friendship is his **only** thought
concerning me

Maybe he already has a significant other..
with whom he's deeply in love

Maybe he's just a man..
among many.. who simply.. fit the profile

Whatever his intentions..
whatever his thoughts are of me..
where ever his heart
is taking him concerning me..

I believe that he is genuine..
I've seen it in his eyes
when he's looked at me

Erika D. Newton

Whether it be friendship
or something more, with him...
my heart believes that he is sincere

I wonder what he would say
if he knew this poem were about him..
Would he feel awkward?
Would he think I was certifiable?
Would he chuckle and say..
'Aww.. how cute!'?

Would he feel sorry for me
and try to think of something to say
to avoid hurting my feelings??

Or..

Would he open up **his** book
& show me a poem
that he wrote about me?

These are simply... thoughts
running across my heart..
Which I felt impelled
to transfer onto paper.

In the years to come..
I expect to look back at this...
& smile at the long gone memory
of this particular..

Someone

"Don't Wanna"

I don't wanna kiss you
while all of this is still new
Because I'd rather be kissing **you**..
than kissing my concocted **idea** of you

When I know you deep...
When you know me deep
Our kiss will be meaningful, intentional,
a genuine faith leap

If now you say you love me..
tell me.. how can that be?
You barely know **of** me

Your conversation is deep..
like I'm your one & only
You say you like my style..
you like the way that I flow
but you have yet to see..
how deep my waters really go

Every word you pour out to me
can only be based on the superficiality
you see on my surface
We haven't even had lunch together..
what's really your purpose?

You looked me deep into my eyes..
& said you'd give me your first... & your last
Stop telling me you love me..
You're moving way too fast

Yes.. I love you.. with the love of Christ
But I don't know you well enough
to love you with my whole life

Not to say that one day..
you and me.. can't be.. see..
If God made you .. for **me**..
then together we will be

But I gotta let you know..
cuz I refuse to be a phony
I'm horizontally disabled
until holy matrimony

So..

If you're vertically challenged
in the way of truly lovin me
You best keep walkin Mista Man..
cuz you're not worthy
of the blessing that is me

But I've gotta admit...

You are causing things to stir
in the depths of my soul
The butterflies.. the rapid heartbeat..
Thoughts that I don't wanna control

You say you love me 100% spirit..
and not according to your flesh
If God confirms your words....
Time will write the rest

But.. until then...
I don't wanna kiss you
while all of this is still new
Because..

I'd rather be kissing **you**..
than kissing my concocted **idea** of you

"You"

You poured out your heart tonight..
shared a bit of your soul
You allowed me to visit with your spirit..
as your words took control

I must admit..
your secret place was warm to my heart..
and very much inviting

I imagined a life with you..
the joy of being in your arms..
Even the making up after the fighting

You said..
you could love me without touching...

You said..
"I love you with a devotion & dedication
that will continue to grow
until I pass from this existence"..

You prayed for me.. for all that is mine
& for every one of those
who are close to me

It would be entirely too easy
to fall in love with the 'you'
that you **appear** to be

You visually portray
everything I need in a man... But

After you've held my hand
a thousand times..
will you stand... still?

I don't know if you can..
much less if you will

I believe that God sent you..
because His word is engraved in your heart
But is it just for a season?
A fleeting moment in divine time?

Or could it be a deeper reason..
like maybe you're supposed to be mine?

If He sent you
to be nothing more than my friend..

then..

my heart has already betrayed me...
because I desire you more now..
than I desired you then

Only one thing could extinguish the fire
in my heart for you
That is to discover that..
you are not the you I **thought** I knew

If you are not ready..
to love one and only **this** one..
If you are not ready..
to turn your back on the moon
and run towards the Son

If you are not ready..
to spend your life
with your one true wife

Then.. simply put..
you are not qualified to walk with me
Nor are you worth my sacrifice

Floetic Ascension of a Lotus

My plan is to do
every bit of what my Father commands

In His love, on His word, in His presence..
in holy purity, I will forever stand

I must admit.. I want with fervent desire..
for you to be my God-sent man
But I will wait, trust God.. & lean not
to what I do or do not understand

Yes...

You poured out your heart tonight..
shared a bit of your soul
You allowed me to visit with your spirit..
as your words took control

But.. are you genuine?

I hope that you are sincere..
I pray that you are not carrying
the motives of a wolf after the sheep

Because you..

if God wills..

are the one

I'd like

To...

keep

Erika D. Newton

"In My Belly"

Deep in my belly..
you accommodate much space

You sit there.. you play there..
you run it like you own the place

You even sent your butterflies..
several it seems

I can feel the passion
through the incessant flutter
of their wings

The words that I carry
from my belly to my heart for you
Are softer and more insistent
than whispers on the wind

The memory of your touch..
with the anticipation of another..
Gives my heart a sweet, beautiful sound
as it beats to your rhythm

To deny the intensity
of the effect you are having on me
Would be...

unadulterated fallacy..
A useless effort of futility
See...

Floetic Ascension of a Lotus

The rivers of expectation
that you flow into me..
spill over the brim..

Effectively!!

The tender essence
of you in Him.. and Him in you
Persuasively caresses me..
Expertly permeates me

Drenching me in the soft fluidity
of your spiritual warmth

Sending powerful bursts of heavenly desire
Directly to.. and straight through..
the very marrow of my being

Body, soul & spirit
affectionately penetrated
by the arrow of your meaning

Within pure walls of angelic solitude..
my breathing resonates

My inhales & exhales balance
as my spirit divinely fixates

On He Who is above.. *remembering*
that only His Holy Love
truly satiates... but

Erika D. Newton

I am lost inside of
my shameless desire of you

because it *appears* that...

His Love.. graces your entire being
oh so magnificently

His word flows from your heart
through your mouth
in great, sure measure

Your faith marches
to the cadence of His Majesty

His supreme glory
shines through your spirit

& this is beauty to be treasured

YES.. Deep in my belly..
you accommodate much space

You sit there.. you play there..
you run it like you own the place

You even sent your butterflies..
several it seems

I can feel the passion
through the incessant flutter
of their wings

Floetic Ascension of a Lotus

"Lord, If You Sent Him"

Lord.. if You sent him..
If You will this to be
forgive me and send him again..
command that he come unto me
If You send him back to me, I will know
that You fashioned him.. especially for me

In the very moment..
that he looked into my eyes
he took my hand & brought it to his lips
my heart skipped beats & I
was taken by surprise.. when he said...

"I love you..
with a devotion and dedication
that will continue to grow..
until I pass from this existence"

I opened up my mouth to respond...
but what escaped
was cloaked in metaphorical nonsense
My words didn't line up
with the beat of my heart

As I looked into the eyes
of this man of God sitting across from me
I did not understand..
or perhaps simply did not believe..
that the truth engraved in my marrow
would have truly set me free

His words were like..
a heated blanket to my soul
Like rivers of warm waters
caressing me from head to toe

His kiss.. I hoped.. was from God..
a long time awaited
His heart embraced mine..
and I was spiritually elated

This beautiful man.. came into my life
with a spirit oh so bold
Ready.. so ready..
to be the husband I prayed for

But my faith in that area..
was pure – ice – cold
My emotions got the best of me..
and I closed that door

Now I sit here.. alone
wondering what could have been
Missing him, needing him..
wanting it all to begin again

Father,
You see where I am..
You see where & with whom
You've called me to be

If You manifest the opportunity..
I will tell him the truth.. that I love him
That with him, in You,
is where I ache to be

Lord.. if You sent him..
If You will this to be
forgive me and send him again..
command that he come unto me

If You send him back to me, I will know
that You fashioned him.. especially for me

He came back..
but little did I know…
the enemy.. 'the inner me'
would use my desperate plea..
to preserve a space for me..
"On Death's Bed"

Erika D. Newton

"On Death's Bed"

My heart was led astray..
By the enemy within the inner me
I did not wait on God
My soul I followed in the wrong direction
When I lay on death's bed

He said he loved me..
That he needed a strong woman
In his corner
That he was looking for a wife
And may have found her.. in me
I believed him..
And I lay on death's bed

He looked into my eyes &
Poured false sincerity into my marrow
He held me.. touched me.. & kissed me
I thought I needed him
As I lay on death's bed

My flesh wants to blame him..
This Minister of the gospel

Because..

Though I resisted and
Repeatedly mouthed the word no...

Partially uncovered..
God's temple was violated
As I was painfully penetrated
While I lay on death's bed

The second time...
I resisted him not

Floetic Ascension of a Lotus

A willing participant
Intertwined against His will
Commingling with unholy desire

In death defying diligence
Yet.. pleasure was non-existent
As I lay on death's bed

I allowed myself
To fall into temptation
In the hopelessness
Of gaining his affection...

In my direct disobedience
I placed man above God..
I placed 'What If' above His Holy Love
Leaving hell on the throne
As I lay on death's bed

Lord.. it hurts to seek Your face
Knowing that Your Name
I have disgraced
I heeded Your voice not

I repent in truth.. &
From my sin I turn away
For Your grace and mercy I ask
Please forgive me
Cleanse me from all
Unrighteousness acquired
As I lay on death's bed

The Minister said I misunderstood
His confession of love for me
He said... he simply loved me
With the love of Christ...
That he has confessed this same love
To hundreds of others...

Broken hearted I write
Trying to see the good God promised

Thanking Him in everything
Even in this.. Wishing that I

Could take back
That very first kiss

Father.. forgive him too
Cleanse him and make him new
Whiter than snow.. as only You can do

Lord.. I forgive him.. I forgive myself
& I cast my cares on You

The devil is a LIAR
He wants to destroy my heart

Yea

Though I have fallen..
I will not play the 'Woe is me' charade

Condemnation withers beneath me
Because.. from God's Love
Nothing can separate me

So I shake myself from the dust
Leaving the old man dead behind me
To walk after the Spirit of Life

Knowing that in His way..
I cannot be mislead
The way that I was

When I lay on death's bed

The immensity of your life's mission
Is carried by Divine provision
Therefore.. uninhibited by worldly condition

Live According To His MIGHT In You

Chapter Six

⋙ Inspirational Discoveries ⋘

1.} In Dreams

2.} Beauty of a Sunset

3.} What Is a Friend

4.} Beauty Is

5.} Beyond the Ozone

6.) Dreams Are

Floetic Ascension of a Lotus

"In Dreams"

In dreams..

Prophetic freedom reigns un-harnessed
Flying without wings is a simple feat..
almost too easily accomplished

In dreams..

The impossible is only possible..
and is always so
The moment I think it.. I become it
The places I imagine..
are where I effortlessly go

In dreams..

The sun is brighter.. and its rays burn not
The moon bursts forth with its radiant light
swimming across its earthly lot

In dreams..

I've risen in flight, surpassing time & space..
I've fallen below the depths of
death's ability to discern

In dreams..

I am everything I strive to be...
magnified beyond measure
I move on purpose, in Divine purpose

In dreams

"Beauty of a Sunset"

So beautiful it is.. A perfect orb
Its soft rays of light radiating through
deep luminous shades of pinks & purples

Majestically positioned against the sky,
prizmatically displaying its flawless elegance
as it graces the edge of the sea
with its presence

Penetrating the atmosphere with its warmth
as it extends beyond itself
Expertly embracing me.. caressing my skin
as it permeates my very being

Its brilliance dances with the wind...
causing the slightly toasted breeze
to envelope me in swirls

It is as if the breath of God is traveling down
from heavens open window
Quickening the marrow within

The beauty of a sunset

"What Is A Friend"

Like the Good Book Says...

A friend loves at all times
And is born, as a 'sister',
For adversity

She is not only loves you
when times are good..

but she loves & is ever there for you
when times are rough..

A friend is silently there
when you need someone to just listen
Is not impatiently waiting to
put in their two cents..

A friend is there
to help you pick up the pieces
when your life shatters around you..

A friend is someone who truly loves you
and does not judge you
as the world does..

A true friend forgives you
when you've hurt their feelings..

and a true friend

will acknowledge and apologize
when they've hurt yours..

A real friend will tell you the truth..
Like if you have spinach in your teeth..

Erika D. Newton

Or if you have that white stuff gathered
at the corners of your mouth

A friend will tell you
if another woman
has been observing your man..

Will help clean up the vomit
when you get sick..

Ok well..
maybe that's taking it a bit far..

BUT, she will at least
grab you a towel & a garbage bag!!

A friend laughs with you
cries with you, suffers with you
and rejoices with you

A friend.. a true friend..
Does not blow away
like withered leaves in the wind..

She is like the palm tree...
strong and majestic
staying deeply rooted
in true love for you

Through every season...
Through the fires...
& through all the storms of life

Like the Good Book Says...

A friend loves at all times
And is born, as a 'sister',
For adversity

"Beauty Is..."

It should move you
that heaven's children stand before you
more in touch with the significance
of their God given beauty
than those of the world could ever fathom

Beauty is reflected from within

It is not merely...

How pearly white & straight your teeth are
How flawless your skin is.. or
How round your hips are..

It is not measured by the sway
or lack thereof..
in your **'Get it girl'** walk

It is not about..
how tall or short or lean or thick you are..
or how provocatively you can
Rip the Runway

It is said that
Beauty is in the eye of the beholder..

I submit to you...
that if the beholder
does not have Godly revelation
concerning the true definition of... 'Beauty'

Then.. the eye of that beholder
does not exist

Erika D. Newton

Beauty is in the soul of a happy child..

Beauty is in the tear
that fell from the heart
which not only **looked upon**
But **moved** in opposition **to**..
another's distress

Beauty is in the sound
of a baby's first cry
fresh from his mother's womb

After purity has been stolen
and dignity has been violated...
Beauty is in the redeemed voice
boldly proclaiming

"I'm Still Standing!"

Beauty is the infrastructure of
more than a conqueror

It is strength.. it is perseverance..
it is passion.. it is fearless.. it is Truth

Beauty is deliberately authentic..

It is a force.. internally driven
by Love, in Love & through Love

Beauty is visible
through **from** the nucleus
of its possessor

Beauty reigns from within..

shamelessly

"Beyond the Ozone"

Somewhere beyond the ozone...

Past where the edge of the sea
meets the sky

Life blows its tender kisses
through the atmosphere
directly to me

I will let not one..
fall to the ground unclaimed

Its travel time
from the Lips of its Origin
to the cheeks of my life...
to the lips of my soul...

was

Divinely determined
before the foundation of the earth

The intensity of its impact
controlled by the weather of my tone

And is driven.. by the wind
in the conviction of my words

Erika D. Newton

"Dreams Are"

Dreams are an abyss of pleasures..
A spiritual treasure chest
Subliminally chained.. consciously denied

Vivid details sharply accentuated

Colors magnified beyond the ability
Of natural sight to comprehend

Abnormal normalities
Woven with such
Perfectly understood intricacy

Dreams are peaceful surrender..
Resting at a magnitude
deeper than reality Is able to imitate

They are a depth of relaxation
Providing a comfort
Softer than mere words could ever describe

They are Bliss….
Softer than even the sweetest thought
Of the perfect kiss

Serenity unparalleled

Dreams are tranquil waters
Flowing in cascades of a beauty
the human eye will never…
Because it can never…

See

If God has called me to do it..
It has already been done
For He knows the end from the beginning..
And in Him..
My victory.. is already won

Chapter Seven
⇛ Floetic Haiku ⇚

1.} Church Without Walls

2.} My Question Is This

3.} Memories Long Gone

4.} I've Got What It Takes

5.) Wicked Steward

"Church Without Walls"

To shut yourself in
Putting walls up around you
Keeps Holiness out

Locks wickedness in
You are the Church Without Walls
Let God breathe through you

Others need to see
Who the Lord and Savior is
Some do not know Him

His lost sheep seek Him
Do not hinder their vision
Let your light shine bright

Open up your heart
Testify of His goodness
His mercy, His grace

His favor, His Blood
His unconditional Love
Go preach the gospel

Go tell all the world
The Lion Of Judah Reigns
Jesus Christ Is Lord

Wake up and get up
Look beyond the distraction
To the Higher things

The chains are broken
You are who God says you are
You were made to shine

Your heart knows full well
Our Savior is alive
He speaks, moves & loves

God loves the world so!
Let His Love inside of you
Pour out upon it

You are dead to sin
You are the Church Without Walls
Let God breathe through you

"My Question Is This"

My question is this
What do I look like to You?
Can You see Your Face?

Do I reflect You?
Are You in the words I speak?
Do I make You proud?

Lord, what do You see
When You look inside my heart?
Can You see Your Love?

What about my life
Am I where I need to be?
Are my steps Your own?

Will I ever hear
Well done my faithful servant
When You speak to me?

Father, answer this
Have I ever made you laugh
Deep from the belly?

Have you ever cried
Because of something that I
Thought, spoke or believed?

Sometimes I wonder
What it is like to be You
So strong, so mighty

Then I remember
You set me apart for You
Covered me in You

Father God tell me
What is it like to watch me?
So close yet so far?

My question is this
What do I look like to You?
Can You see Your Face?

Floetic Ascension of a Lotus

"Memories Long Gone"

Memories long gone
Haunt the corners of my mind
Trying to find me

Kiss me in my heart
That I might feel your glory
And know love is real

There is none like You
In absolute reverence
I bow and submit

Never let me go
There is no me without You
Keep me, lest I die

Screaming from within
As my faith is purified
Glad to be in Love

You are all of me
You are the hope in my tears
The Life in my years

Erika D. Newton

The beat of my heart
You are the kick to my drum
The breath in my lungs

The pep in my step
You are the scope of my dreams
I am drenched in You

When distraction pulls
Preoccupied thoughts tempt me
To forget Your face

Visions of the past
Which You do not remember
Try to catch my stare

Memories long gone
Haunt the corners of my mind
Trying to find me

"I've Got What It Takes"

I've got what it takes
To blaze through the storms of life
Victoriously

When strife strikes my soul
I let Him renew my mind
He built me to last

I stand up in Christ
Blessed and bearing Holy fruit
In Royal High Class

As I move through life
Walking in authority
I take my stuff back

Speak when spoken through
Echo what He says to you
Hear the word **and** do

Walking in His Love
Planting seeds and saving souls
Is true victory

Erika D. Newton

There is none greater
He moves in the Trinity
God is Almighty

His whole Life is mine
I am covered in His Blood
Jesus Christ chose me

Nothing can stop me
His Power pulls me forward
Past the enemy

He reaches through me
Pulling lost souls unto Him
By testimony

I've got what it takes
To blaze through the storms of life
Victoriously

Floetic Ascension of a Lotus

"Wicked Steward"

I did not listen
I was a wicked steward
Therefore I was poor

I had no money
Could not even buy water
I reaped what I sowed

I beat on my chest
At the hurt I caused my God
Hating all my sin

Hot tears streaked my cheeks
As I cried out in sorrow
LORD, help me to change

O' wicked am I
I lay broken before You
I deserve to die

His Voice answered me:
RISE to a New Covenant
Bound in Love & grace

My Lord now proclaims:
Your sins are forgiven you
Receive Righteousness

Abba, I have failed
Was not wise with the little
Now I have nothing

I remain faithful
My Grace far outweighs your sin
Only trust in me

Abba, my heart breaks
I was disobedient
I have let you down

**Stand upon My Word
Receive no condemnation
Believe in My Son**

Lord, where shall I go
And by what means shall I live
What if my heart fails

**I shall lead the way
I will supply ALL your need
Your heart is made new**

Father who am I
That You should look upon me
And pour out such grace

**My Son is right here
Interceding for your life
His Blood makes you whole**

Abba, Yahweh, Lord
I do not deserve this grace
Yet You make it mine

**Freely I give it
And if you freely receive
You shall overcome**

Christ, my Savior Lives!
The Finished Work of the Cross
Gives grace & makes right!

Believe the Good News!

*Truly I tell you, whoever does not
receive and accept and welcome
the kingdom of God
like a little child does
positively shall not enter it at all*

Chapter Eight
⇛ Let the Children Come ⇚

1.} Janeyah's Poem

2.} I Belong

3.} Beautiful Ray of Light

4.} I Like Me

5.} You Cannot

6.} A Real Princess

"Janeyah's Poem"

God made me

God made you

Some eyes brown

Some eyes blue

We're all different

We're all beautiful too

Because we're all made
by the same Hands

YEAH!!!

"I Belong"

To HIM I Belong..

HE is the reason why I breathe
Why I smile.. why I laugh

HE is the reason why I hope
why I dream.. why I move

HE is the reason why I suffer
with patience & endurance

HE is my Strength, My Rock,
My Shield, My Shepherd
He is the One Who gave me Life

He prepared a place for ME In Him..
at the Right hand of Almighty GOD

My Lord gave me victory eternal..
delivering me from the curse of Adam..
Unto the Blessing of the Christ

My Lord took me from death..
So that I may Live... abundantly

My Lord loves Me.. so very deeply

He Is my Life & my life Is His

To Him I Belong..

Floetic Ascension of a Lotus

"Beautiful Ray of Light"

In this life, I will be tested

I will face challenges
I will face frustrations
I will face haters

But in Christ,

I am **more** than a conqueror!
& even when I fall short..
God sees me as a winner!
Therefore...

I ALWAYS WIN!!

In times of sadness & in times of pain
I will not forget Him who sent me

In times of joy & in times of prosperity
I will not forget Him who chose me

God is Love.. God lives in me
Therefore – I am Love
I walk in love, I speak in love,
I operate completely in
& can only function in.. Love

Gods Love in me is His light in me
He shines so brightly through me
The world can't help but see that...

I am a beautiful ray of light

Sent by God

Erika D. Newton

"I Like Me"

When I look into the mirror
What do I see?
I see **me**
From the top of my head
To the bottom of my feet

Let me tell you **just** why I like me

Before I was born
God thought about me
He chose my parents
& the color of these eyes you see

He counted every hair
Before he put them on my head
& before I made a sound
He knew every word I ever said

He knew I'd like to dance
He knew I'd like to sing
& He knew that at the park
My favorite thing would be the swing

When God made me
He knew from the very start
The exact day Jesus would come
To live in my heart

Jesus teaches me lots of things
Like how to be brave...

Floetic Ascension of a Lotus

Like how to smile when I'm sad
& how to behave

He teaches me about love..
About how to give & how to help

He teaches me how to look up
When I feel alone..

So that I'm never by myself

Yes God shaped ME
With His own two hands
He gave me my skin, my smile
& the legs on which I stand

But what I like best
Is what He put inside
It's the Power and the Love
Where His Holy Spirit resides!

When somebody makes me mad
& I feel like being mean
The Holy Spirit says

'Hey...

That's playing for the wrong team'

So I lean on the Holy Spirit
& I let Him make me nice
No no.. it's not easy...

Just ask Jesus Christ!

But He gave me His Word
That I would always win
If Him only would I serve

And to Him I say YES!
Even during hard times
Because if I never give up
If I let the smile in my heart shine..

In the end, everyone will see
What a good job God did
When He made me!

So...

When *I* look into the mirror
What do I *see*?

I see **me**
From the top of my head
To the bottom of my feet!

& Now you know **just** why

I LIKE ME!!

Floetic Ascension of a Lotus

"You Cannot"

You cannot know who you are
Without first knowing Who He is

                                    You cannot represent the Truth
                                      By displaying yourself as a lie

You cannot see.. without a vision

                                           You cannot persevere
                                      In a gift you refuse to activate

You cannot determine to finish something
You never had the courage to start

                                   You cannot manifest a dream
                                             You refuse to pursue

You cannot fulfill your divine destiny
Without knowing your divine purpose

                                    You cannot master the thing
                                        You refuse to be taught

You cannot run before you walk,
You cannot walk before you stand.. and
You cannot stand **strong**.. without first rising in Him

                                  You cannot find your true self
                           Without first allowing God to find you

Because...

You cannot know who you are
Without first knowing Who He is

"A Real Princess"

I am a Real Princess..
Because my Father is the Real King
Oh goodness no.. I am not a fairytale
Oh Heavens Yes! I am the Real Thing

The Christ Who lives inside of me
Is better than Cinderella, Tinkerbell or Mulan
For they are merely folklore
My Christ is Real.. & He needs no wand

The existence of existence
Every adjective, noun & verb
Was created by the King of kings
Through the utterance of His Word

In His Royal Grace
He placed a Crown atop my head
Setting me apart as His own.. &
This is what He Said

I crown you blessed, I crown you wise
I crown you 'Apple of My Eye'
I crown you fearfully & wonderfully made
I crown you daughter.. For you are Mine

King of kings.. Lord of lords
That's Who my Father is
Though there may be kings on earth
No throne sits higher than His... Therefore,

I *am* a **Real Princess**..
Because my Father

is the **Real King**!

*Thoughtless thoughts
are not lacking in power…
Be effective, not defective.
Renew your mind*

Chapter Nine
⋙ The Truth About Love ⋘

1.} Smile and Nod

2.} I Thank You Lord

3.} Love

4.} How To Find A Husband

5.} Lord.. I Love You

6.} This Love

7.} Never Let Me Go

Floetic Ascension of a Lotus

"Smile and Nod"

Everything is so *hush hush*
Can't say this.. don't speak that
Don't you dare ever vocalize
What some of those voices inside whisper
Just smile and nod... smile and nod

Attempting to discern this silence
Above the ruckus in my brain
Is like trying to hear the silk of
Summer rain as it slides through
Midair - *in vain*! so I just
Smile and nod... smile and nod

If technology developed the ability to
Audibly express mortal thoughts..
The world would become afraid of itself
Shaking on its axis
With every petrified turn..
No longer could we hide as we
Smile and nod... smile and nod

There is One.. Who knows us all
Who hears every thought plain as day..
From the pinnacle of the purest..
To the bowels of the most abhorrent

But me.. He has eternally forgiven
He remembers my sins no more
His Spirit convicts me unto Righteousness
Forever sealing me in the redeeming Blood
I trust Him.. because in spite of myself..
He loved me first.. &

In Him I stand protectively exposed as I
Smile and nod... smile and nod

"I Thank You Lord"

By the grace of God
I can spread my wings and soar
I can spread them out and fly
Like I've never flown before

He touched my soul
Like it ain't been touched before
His Love.. it flows through me
Infiltrating me through the core

By the strength of His Hand
My knees are on the floor
Tears of joy streak my face
As I praise my Lord

When I call on Your Name
You put Your eyes on me... &
You show me things
That I could not before see

Because You love me
Your mercy follows me
& Your grace is new every day

Floetic Ascension of a Lotus

& I want the entire world to see!

Without You as my Life
Where would I be?
Chained down in the dark
Unable to see

Through my veins
You flow so gracefully
My soul You bought
When You Bled for me

Oh Lord.. help me to NEVER forget
The price You paid for me
That You are the reason I shall live
For all of eternity

And I thank You Lord
Yes I thank You Lord
For Loving Me

Oh how I thank You Lord
Yes.. I thank You Lord.. &
I Love You Too!

"Love"

A Love
stronger than the mightiest wind..
more passionate than
I have ever experienced..

Is engraved.. forever imprinted..
in, on & drenched throughout
my spirit.. my innermost being

Only when I am still
Can He penetrate my true essence..
the very substance of me

And..

Only when I am focused upward
Can I bathe in and be taken by..
That Holy.. Divine..
Uncompromised Love.. He is beautiful

To know that He sincerely,
thoroughly & unconditionally
loves **me**.. satiates me
with an immeasurable magnitude
of pure, unadulterated joy ..

And as a consequence..
Reminds me of how utterly cold it is
outside of Him

An unbreakable.. undeniable Love
so sweet and undiluted
Has touched me in the nucleus
of my immortal existence..

A Love
So completely powerful that...

it brings me to tears
Tears of exaltation, tears of reverence..
Tears of gratitude.. Tears of Awe..
and of deep.. deep.. peace

Tears which stream down my face
in triumph, hope.. and security

The beauty of His Love
runs so deep that..
It cannot be seen by the natural eye

It can only be experienced
when you surrender your naked..
Vulnerable.. fragile self to Him..
in unrestrained totality

Pureness of heart.. is the window
through which God will enter..
And through which you will perceive
and receive His glory.

The fullness of Him will flow through you..
With such divine perfection,
that it will leave you without words..

His presence stripping you
of the ability to doubt..
The undeniable Truth
of His existence

"How to Find a Husband"

I found my Husband in Isaiah 54:5..
The Lord of Hosts is His Name
My Maker is alive

For my husband in the earth..
I have no need to look.. because...

He who finds a **wife**, finds a good thing
She who finds a **husband**...
I could not find in the Book

The Lord molds the bride..
Shapes the bride.. and prepares the bride
For the man He has meticulously fashioned
Especially for her

He soaks her through with wisdom
Unconditional Love..
& a sweet aromatic grace

He takes His Holy Waters
& purifies her with Himself
He declares that she is ready
When in her reflection..
He sees His Face

She is willing and full of faith
As she follows His lead
She walks the narrow road..
Planting the Life-giving seed

Floetic Ascension of a Lotus

She is in love with the Lord
& God is well pleased
That though her heart
Desires a husband in the earth

Her focus is set on honoring His will..
In word and in deed

And because she knows.. that God will
Give her the desires of her heart
She studies how to be the wife
God intended from the start

She walks by faith..
In prudence, honor and respect
Aware that how she submits to her Maker..
Is how she ought to submit
To the husband she would one day get

So.. she ushers in the Spirit..
NOW she sets the atmosphere
That holiness and purity should remain
Even *after* her husband gets here

Her sent man will find her..
As their divine paths meet
He will see her.. and he will know her..

Because

God has already ordered the direction
Of his heartbeat

Erika D. Newton

She will be **prepared**
to be the God-ordained wife

She will edify him.. as she edifies Christ
She will exalt him.. as she exalts Christ
She will commit herself unto him

As unto the Lord..
For the rest of her earthly life

She will boldly proclaim
What thus Says the Lord

"My husband is worthy of my praise..
Of my reverence and veneration!
I admire him exceedingly..
Respect him greatly
I will withhold NONE of my affection

Lord.. help me to live Your word
In everything I do.. and in everything I say
I desire that in my very poise..
With every graceful step I take
That my husband be glorified..
For Your Holy Name's sake"

And..

The husband will love his wife..
Just as Christ loves the church
Through the ups and the downs..
The joys.. and the hurts

Floetic Ascension of a Lotus

He will give himself up for her..
Will leave his father and his mother

Because..

In her he found a *Real* good thing..
And for him, there is no other
He sees her as a blessing..
& it is his delight
To honor her as holy.. Yes..
She is hallowed in his sight

Although he is the head..
They become one – side by side
That their steps may echo in perfect unison..
With every divinely ordained stride

He will treat her as he treats his own body
Protecting her, cherishing her,
Nourishing her always

Together.. they will hold firm
To the ways of the Lord
Moving forward in His will..
For the rest of their days.

Both husband and wife..
Valuing the Lord above each other
Are mindful.. to keep Him first place
Comprehending that there will never..
Because there could never..

Ever.. Be Another

HOWEVER,
LET EACH MAN OF YOU
(WITHOUT EXCEPTION)
LOVE HIS WIFE
AS BEING IN A SENSE
HIS VERY OWN SELF;
AND LET THE WIFE
SEE THAT SHE RESPECTS AND
REVERENCES HER HUSBAND
{THAT SHE NOTICES HIM,
REGARDS HIM, HONORS HIM.
PREFERS HIM, VENERATES
AND ESTEEMS HIM;
AND THAT SHE DEFERS TO HIM,
PRAISES HIM, AND LOVES
AND ADMIRES HIM
EXCEEDINGLY}

EPHESIANS 5:33 AMP

"Lord.. I Love You"

Lord.. I Love You

You are so amazing
Sometimes.. I just wanna lay back..
And revel in the pure awe of You

There is nothing greater
than to be filled with Your presence

You fill my heart with such
incredible joy and appreciation..

Lord.. You bring my soul
into dumbstruck silence..
with the raw beauty of Your
signs and wonders

I don't have to see You
to know that You are here..
My spirit rejoices
in the magnificence
of Your presence

Thank You Lord...
for loving me so much
that You would take the time to
drench me in Your glory

That You would touch my life so undeniably..
with such precious, holy Light..
Is so breathtakingly beautiful to me

Thank You Lord
that You would touch me deep enough..
to render me speechless

Lord.. I love You..

I acknowledge You
& require You
With every breath I take

Thank You Father
For knowing me by name..
For keeping me..
For visiting your splendor
So graciously upon me

Lord.. I love You
I submit myself to You willingly..
Unabashedly.. completely

You have given me
the capacity to hear & obey..

You have bestowed upon me
Your precious Agape Love
Pouring Yourself without reserve..
In **to** me and out **through** me.. selah

You have bequeathed to me
An Eternal Life.. I, in no way, deserved
Nor will I ever possess the ability to earn
Simply because it was your good pleasure

Ask of me what You will
For nothing You could ever require of me
Will ever compare to Your sacrifice

You are so amazing

Sometimes.. I just wanna lay back..
And revel in the pure awe of You

Floetic Ascension of a Lotus

"This Love"

You are no longer
The center of my universe…

You have been replaced by This Love…
& This Love.. never hurts

You could never compare
To this Love
So abundant.. yet so rare

When you had me..
You constantly evaded me
Always dancing
on the peripheral edge of my sight

But this Love dances with me, in me,
All around & through me
Yeah.. this Love I can see clearly
Especially… with my eyes shut tight

When my focus was you..
I never knew what to expect..
Would you hold me?

Would you even see me?
Or would you leave me crying those
Familiar tears of neglect?

Not this Love.. No No.. NEVER this Love
This Love is beautiful.. warm.. & nice

My tears are dried up
In the joy this Love brings
This Love sings away my fears
in the darkness of the night

When you were mine..
I'd wake up and wonder where you went

This Love.. never lets me go..
For it is heaven sent

You are no longer
The center of my universe...

You have been replaced by This Love...
& This Love.. never hurts

Floetic Ascension of a Lotus

"Never Let Me Go"

You are my Life..
I am nothing outside of You
LORD, Never let me go

I give You **all** of me
I surrender to Your Holiness inside of me
To You and You only Lord... I bow

I desire to please You
'Well done My good & faithful servant'
Are the words I long to hear from You

Cause the strength You have planted in me
to rise up & overflow out of me
That I may fulfill that which You will

Continue working in me,
on me & through me...
Perfecting all that concerns me...
Until I have completed the task
You have entrusted me with O' God

I am not ashamed in my requiring You
Without You I cannot breathe..
let alone stand

You are my Life..
I am nothing outside of You

LORD, **Never** let me go

If I should veer away from the path
You have set before me Lord God

BLOCK MY WAY

Your divine will for my life
is what I seek

Your divine will for my life
is what I speak

Your divine will for my life
is all I need

Your divine will for my life
is all I plead

Whatever the sacrifice... I am Yours
Do what You will... Have Your way

When I hunger... Your word is my food..
Lord, because of You.. I hunger no more

When I thirst... You are my Living Water
Lord, because of You.. I thirst no more

Selah

You are my Life..
I am nothing outside of You

LORD, **Never** let me go

Never again..
Will I allow myself to be cheapened

The Blood which redeemed me is priceless
I am precious, Divine Royalty

Money is not worth me
And..
Neither ignorance nor impurity
Can afford me

Chapter Ten
➽ **Shut Up & Live** ➽

1.} Woman, Get Up

2.} Immersion

3.} When You Come Back

4.} Ventilated Truth

5.} Matters

6.} Your Move

Floetic Ascension of a Lotus

"Woman, Get Up"

Woman.. take your life back
Get out from under death's oppressive lie

Your true nature is power
Heavily soiled with divine capability
Weakness can no longer suffocate you
Breathe in the authority bequeathed to you
Woman.. Yes You Can

)))))))) **BLACK WOMAN, *GET UP*** ((((((((

Shut your voice to excuses that cripple you
Close your thoughts
to reasonings that bind you

Lies are expensive..
Believing them can cost you your life

Darkness has paraded
on your back so long that
Bloody shoe prints defile the ground
Beneath your breasts

Rise NOW.. and take firm hold
Of the Mighty Hand outstretched toward you

You are royalty redeemed
Bought back at a price
No earthly riches could ever bestow

Though you were never worth the Blood
He decided the Blood was worth you
Get up.. NOW.. and take your dignified stand
Black woman.. Yes You Can

))))))))) **WHITE WOMAN, *GET UP*** (((((((((

How long will you lay broken
Atop and fixed within the rubble of self pity..

Refuse to any longer
lie motionless in prostration
Your back towards the Son

Spit the dust from your mouth and **RISE** – *'Sista'*
Tilt back your head and allow the Light
To penetrate your blind eyes
Filling you with the insight
Of who you really are

Though you were never worth the Blood
He decided the Blood was worth ***you***
Get up.. NOW.. and take your dignified stand
White woman.. Yes You Can

))))))))) **YOUNG WOMAN, *GET UP*** (((((((((

Your teardrops are like glass
Encasing your soul
Flowing in a costly fragility
Your spirit cannot afford

They trickle down your face and
Shatter as they hit the ground

The bitterness of you now lying in shards
Waiting impatiently to draw the blood
Of anyone who dares try
To put you back together again

Rise NOW.. with righteous indignation
Look up and see the Truth of your worth

Floetic Ascension of a Lotus

Let the Healer of the broken hearted
Love you like no other could ever
Develop the ability to

If you allow Him, He will re-create you
Unshakeable, Irreplaceable, & Un-breakable

Though you were never worth the Blood
He decided the Blood was worth you
Get up.. NOW.. and take your dignified stand
Young woman.. Yes You Can

)))))))) **OLD WOMAN, *GET UP* ** (((((((((

Why have you enabled your senses
To become anesthetized by
Prolonged periods of poorly governed time

By choice – you are here
&...
Only by choice – will you remain

Rise NOW.. from your stagnation
Rest in it no more
Speak Life into your dry bones

Permit them not to crumple beneath you
Command your feeble limbs to walk by faith
In renewed trust, strength, and dominion

Though you were never worth the Blood
He decided the Blood was worth you
Get up.. NOW.. and take your dignified stand
Old woman.. Yes You Can

))))))))) **GODLY WOMAN, *GET UP* ** (((((((((

That Black Woman.. Needs you
That White Woman.. Needs you
That Young Woman.. Needs you
That Old Woman.. Needs you

That Woman is...
Your mother, your daughter, your sister,
Your Doctor, your bus driver, your teacher
She's your neighbor, she's your best friend

She delivers your mail, cashes your check
She sits next to you at church
You look into her eyes across the counter
as she takes your order

)))))))) **GODLY WOMEN, *GET UP*** ((((((((

IT IS **HARVEST** TIME!

That woman is ripe.. we must sow into her
Life Seed from our Father's Garden

)))))))) **GODLY WOMEN, *GET UP*** ((((((((

That woman was once you
How **DARE** you not fight for you!

Woman.. take your life back
Get out from under death's oppressive lie
Your true nature is power
Heavily soiled with divine capability
Weakness can no longer suffocate you
Breathe in the authority bequeathed to you

ALL YE WOMEN...

)))))))))) ***GET UP!!!*** ((((((((((

"Immersion"

Immersion is the only solution..

To be submerged in You..
The Living Water
Is the answer to my problematic woes

The Love of Your flow
Buries my cries
Drowning out death's lies

I am alive in You
As I rise with Your tide

Breathing You deep.. filling my veins
Saturating my wounds
The seepage lost in Your waves

))))))) JEHOVAH RAPHA!!!! ((((((

Healer of my broken heart
Redeemer of my broken soul..

Envelope me and soak me through
Absorb my marrow.. replace it with You
Embrace me.. YES.. bathe me in You

Revelation falls like rain as I
Meditate in the still depths of You
My pain is washed away
As You wade me through

Let the rivers of Your heart purify me
As You pour Love down..

Ceaselessly

Erika D. Newton

"When You Come Back"

When You come back for me..
May You find me loving You
With all my heart, soul & strength
And loving my neighbor
As I love myself

Oh Father.. May You find me
Pressing faithfully toward the mark
Walking diligently in Your footsteps

If I am on my knees at Your return..
May You find me praying
For the happiness of my enemies
May You find me sincerely blessing
Those who curse me

When You come back for me..
May You find Your double-edged sword
Being righteously wielded from my mouth
From the foundation of Christ – My Savior

May Your nostrils be pleasantly satiated
With the fragrance of my worship
With the potent authenticity of my praise

OH LORD.. How elated I would be!!
If You were to look upon my face
& see Your reflection! If You would declare of me
'Well done My good & faithful servant!..
In you I am well pleased!'

May You find me awake & looking for You
Let me never take for granted..
That You Yourself have made me Holy..
& have consecrated me unto You

Floetic Ascension of a Lotus

When You come back for me..
May You find me on **FIRE** for You..
My heart set ablaze with Your Love

Not for a single solitary moment
Can I tolerate even the thought...
Of You finding me lukewarm

For it would destroy me Lord Jesus,
If You were to so much as consider
Spewing me from Your mouth

If upon Your return..
You should look away from me..
If Your Spirit should be grieved of me..

Have enough mercy on me
To graciously remove my teeth...
Lest they be among those gnashing

Upon your arrival LORD
May You find in my heart
Nothing of myself stored there
Nothing of this world hidden there

Find no soul left behind to suffer
In darkness on my account
As the result of my failure
To shed Your precious Light within me

When You come back for me..
May You find me loving You
With all my heart, soul & strength

And loving my neighbor
As I love myself

"Ventilated Truth"

Ventilated truth is not always
Music to the ears

But...

When rooted in the Word of God...
It is a release in the spirit of the speaker
And a conviction in the heart of the hearer
Who chooses to receive

Ventilated truth is not always
Sweet to the taste,

But...

It is the Word Bearer
Reigning in consecrated people
Causing wisdom to be spoken & understood
It is freedom in its most potent form
And prosperity is its substance

Ventilated truth is not always
Pleasing to the eye

But...

It brings about purposeful change
In the one seeking that which is above
Spiritual maturity is the inevitable result
As glory is permitted to manifest

Ventilated truth originates in Love
Perfect in its work

"Matters"

What matters?

The hair wrapped within
the bristles of the brush...

Does it really?

The stain in the wooden table
That just won't come out?

Does it really?

What about the anointing on your life...
Coupled with the word of your testimony
does *IT* matter...

Really?

The woman who has lost her soul
In physical abuse might think so...
What if your heart contains a seed
That would've caused her to overcome..
But it never goes before her eyes..

Will that matter?

What about the child
Who was violated & knows no love?

What if my experiential understanding of
God's Love through my own defilement
Could change him... or her?
But.. that child never hears me..

Would that matter?

Erika D. Newton

What if I chose
To never utter another sound..
Or write another word

What if this precious seed given me
By He Who *IS* Love...
Is buried alongside me?

Will that matter?

When God shows you your life...
Will He show you the souls you skipped over?

Will He show me the hearts I have failed?

Will He open the bag of seed which
He Himself Spoke into our spirits...
Only to find unplanted seed remaining?

Will that matter? Really?

It MATTERS..
All of it matters

PROFOUNDLY

Share the Love of God..

More people than you know..
Still don't know.. & are waiting
With hearts ripe to receive
That specially marked seed
Which is meant to come through you

Does that matter...

To you?

Floetic Ascension of a Lotus

"Your Move"

When He gives you innovative ideas..
You must innovate

When He inspires you with creative insight
You must create

When He ignites you with dynamic ability
You are the dynamite that must go

!!BOOM!!

Exploding onto the scene of your...
Innovatively creative, dynamically ignited

P – U – R – P – O – S – E

**Do you not know that in Christ..
you are the BOMB?**

You are a force of unstop-ability..
& you have officially been unctioned to

BLOW IT UP!!

Your move

Erika D. Newton

*You must resist that
which is resisting you…
Though you shall bend,
You shall **never** break*

⫸ Floetic Ascension of a Lotus ⫷

Just a wildflower picked from the plains of Sharon
A lotus blossom from the valley pools
Rising only to meet the Son
Whose Love calls me higher

A lotus blossoming in a swamp of weeds
Empowered by the unction of infinite Spirit
Bombarded by the onslaught of circumstance...
Attempting to uproot & discard me

Strengthened by the Living Water
Of He Who compels me to ascend
I am swayed & though not broken –
Against my will I bend, as
Incensed waves relentlessly beat against me

I am violently bruised
& my desire to climb has gone from me
For whenever I determine to progress
This bitterness of life attacks... again & again

Only when I am motionless
Does this rage of the sea subside... but why?
Why is progress resisting me?

The Light within... me, also rests above... me
Commanding me as I still myself below

'Keep your heart stayed on Me' He says
'For I am developing you to maturity'

You must resist that which is resisting you
Though you shall bend, you shall never break

Come to Me, hear My Voice, See My Light
You must climb, you must race,
You must fight the good fight

For I have infiltrated & adorned you
With All of Myself
Yea.. My Blood fills you to the full
til there is none of you left... &

I have anointed your heart
With the voice of My song
To carry you upwards.. where you belong

So... as you **rise**, as you **rise**, as you **RISE**
Above what you see – to meet Me
Serenade me wildflower..
by My Word within your seed

That I may be glorified as I exalt
Your Floetic Ascension dear Lotus

For you are My lotus.. indeed

Floetic Ascension of a Lotus

*For God So Loved the World
That He Gave His Only Begotten Son,
That Whoever Believes In Him
Should Not Perish.. But Have
Everlasting Life*

John 3:16 (NKJV)

Take It Personal...

*For God So Loved **YOU**
That He Gave His Only Begotten Son,
That If **YOU** Believe In Him
YOU Will Not Perish..
But Will Have Everlasting Life*

John 3:16 (Personified)

Erika D. Newton

THE

END

Well... Almost!

*Because if you acknowledge
and confess with your lips
that Jesus is Lord
and in your heart believe
(adhere to, trust in, and rely on the truth)
that God raised Him from the dead,
you will be saved*

❧ Romans 10:9 (Amp) ❧

Receiving Your Salvation

No matter who you are.. if you are reading this, you can receive Jesus into your heart and welcome the Love of God RIGHT THIS MOMENT! You don't have to be in church or with a group of Christians in order to be saved. You can be alone in your car, in a bathroom, in a hotel room or ANYWHERE! Jesus Christ came in the flesh – to die for **your** sins so that **YOU** could have eternal life.. & I am a living, breathing witness – that He'll save you right where you are!

Don't let the fact that you've done a lot of things wrong stop you from receiving your salvation. **Romans 3:23** says ALL have sinned and fall short of the glory of God. In other words.. none of us were '*good enough*' to be saved. Don't sell yourself short by thinking you must '*clean yourself up*' before you can '**qualify**' to be saved. The truth is.. righteousness is a FREE GIFT *(Romans 5:17-19)* & there is NOTHING you can do to earn it! No matter what you've done – God Himself places you in right standing with Himself through your faith in Jesus Christ the moment you BELIEVE **(Romans 3:22)**! If you truly desire in your heart to receive the free gift of eternal life (salvation).. you must be born again, & Jesus is the only way.. there is no other. *(John 3:3-7; 14:6)*.

You receive your salvation simply by confessing Jesus as your Lord, believing in your heart that He died for your sins & that God the Father raised Him from the dead. The bible says in Mark 1:15 & Luke 13:3 Amp that we must repent of our sins & believe the Gospel... but what exactly does it mean to 'repent'?

To repent means to have a change of heart, a change of mind & a change of direction – with abhorrence of your past sins *(see Matthew 4:17 Amp)*.

It does **not** mean that you must recount & verbally confess the specifics of every sin you've ever committed. Jesus knows the truth of your heart.. & if your heart cries out to Him as 'Lord' your sins are forgiven you. In **Luke 23:32-43**, you will see that there were two criminals crucified with Christ. One of the criminals railed at Jesus, saying to Him *'save Yourself & us also if You are the Christ'*. While the other criminal reproved his cohort admonishing him, saying *'do you not even fear God seeing that you too are condemned & suffering the same penalty?'* Can you see his heart toward God in these words? Keep reading.. verses 42-43 read:

> ⁴²Then he said to Jesus, Lord, remember me when You come in Your kingly glory!
>
> ⁴³And He answered him, Truly I tell you, today you shall be with Me in Paradise.

Notice how the criminal simply confesses Jesus as Lord & Jesus welcomes him into 'Paradise' with Himself! This criminal did not verbalize specifics of past sins – nor did he recite some long drawn out prayer to receive Jesus. He repented by having a change of mind, a change of heart, a change of direction & confessing Jesus as 'Lord'!

You will see another beautiful example of the love of Christ in **Luke 7:38-50** where a woman described as *'a social outcast, devoted to sin'* unabashedly displayed her love for Jesus. Her heart cried out to Him as she kissed & anointed His feet.. wetting them with her tears & washing them with her hair. Religious leaders were appalled at the sight of it! Again, notice how there is no verbal account of past sins or the reciting of a specified prayer.. only her heart exposed before the Lord. Take a look at what Jesus says to her in verses 48-50:

⁴⁸ And He said to her, Your sins are forgiven!

⁴⁹Then those who were at table with Him began to say among themselves, Who is this Who even forgives sins?

⁵⁰But Jesus said to the woman, Your faith has saved you; go (enter) into peace [in freedom from all the distresses that are experienced as the result of sin].

Did she specifically ask for forgiveness? Yet – Jesus forgave her of her sins & became her Lord & Savior! Repentance is visible to God in your **heart**!

Religion has complicated matters with a lot of extra stuff.. obviously proven unnecessary by the works of Christ we've seen for ourselves in just these few scriptures.. imagine the many more Truths waiting to be revealed to you!

Religion has blurred the vision of many.. and attempts to crowd the doorway – pushing people **back** from Christ – instead of welcoming people **in** to Him. It's **relationship** Jesus is interested in.. not how religious or mechanical you can be about following rules & regulations. The truth is – God loves you.. and He loves you enough to die for you. You will know Him as He draws you into His love through relationship with Him. Take a seat at His feet & allow Him to envelope you in a soft serene warmth that cannot be experienced outside of Him.. the only thing you have to pay.. is attention!

If you **have** been paying attention so far, you should understand that you can receive Jesus through your heart.. speaking very few words on your own. However, for those who prefer written words, as a step of faith – I have provided the following prayer as a simple guideline.

Floetic Ascension of a Lotus

Salvation Prayer

Lord, You said in Your word that if I confess with my mouth that Jesus is Lord and believe in my heart that You raised Him from the dead, I shall be saved. Therefore, Jesus, I confess that You are Lord.

Lord Jesus, I believe that you died on the cross for my sins and that God the Father raised You from the dead. Lord, I admit that I am a sinner, and I am sorry for every wrong thing I ever did.

Lord, I repent for all of my sins and I ask your forgiveness. I thank You Lord that when I repent, You are faithful and just to forgive me & cleanse me of all unrighteousness.

Jesus, I ask you to come into my heart right now, and be Lord of my life! Jesus, I receive you into my heart as my personal Lord and Savior!

I boldly declare that I am now a New Creation in Christ Jesus, a child of the only True & Living God!

In Jesus' Name, Amen!!

If you said that prayer sincerely from your heart, welcome to the Family!!

Now that you are in Christ.. it is no longer you who lives, but Christ Who lives in you *(Galatians 2:20 Amp)*!!

Though trials & tribulation will still come - you now have the **_guaranteed victory_** in & through Christ Jesus - Who has overcome the world and deprived it of its ability to harm you *(John 16:33 Amp)*!

Begin to read the bible.. I believe that starting with the New Testament will lead you to know & understand the 'Finished work of the Cross'.

If you should decide to begin in the Old Testament – do it with the understanding that the wrath of God does not pertain to you. You are saved by **GRACE**! You are precious in His sight & He loves you more passionately than we could ever love our own children.

When you make a mistake & sin – *and you probably will* – only believe God. His grace & mercy covers you for all of eternity. He will help you.. and **He** will work in you to accomplish what is pleasing in His sight. Focus on God and listen for His voice.. You will begin to see Him move in your life in wonderfully amazing ways!!

Just before Jesus began His ministry, He was baptized in water by John the Baptist *(see Matthew 3:16)*. Since, according to **1 Peter 2:21**, we are to follow His example – water baptism is something you should seek the Lord about. Water Baptism declares to the world that you've made the quality decision to live for the Lord. Going down under the water symbolizes death to the old life – rising up symbolizes resurrection to your new life in Christ Jesus!

I do **not** say that water baptism is *'mandatory to **re**tain or **main**tain your salvation'*. Nothing can separate you from the love of God. If the Lord were to bring you into Paradise with Him this very moment – you will not be turned away for not having been baptized! Simply trust in Jesus as He reveals Himself to you.

Now that you are a believer, let's talk about what it means to be baptized in the Holy Spirit.

Believing Jesus & receiving the Holy Spirit go hand in hand. When Paul (a disciple of Christ) came to a city called Ephesus, he found some other disciples. Let's take a look at their conversation in **Acts 19:2-6** (NKJV).

> ² he said to them, "Did you receive the Holy Spirit when you believed?" So they said to him, "We have not so much as heard whether there is a Holy Spirit."
>
> ³ And he said to them, "Into what then were you baptized?" So they said, "Into John's baptism."
>
> ⁴ Then Paul said, "John indeed baptized with a baptism of repentance, saying to the people that they should believe on Him who would come after him, that is, on Christ Jesus."
>
> ⁵ When they heard this, they were baptized in the Name of the Lord Jesus.
>
> ⁶ And when Paul had laid hands on them, the Holy Spirit came upon them, and they spoke with **tongues** & prophesied.

Jesus says in Acts 1:8 *"But you shall receive **power** when the Holy Spirit comes upon you; and you shall be witnesses to Me...."*

When you are filled with the Holy Spirit, you can speak in new tongues... & though yours is the voice you hear, it is the Holy Spirit Who gives you the utterance. **(Acts 2:4)**. Speaking in tongues is nothing to be afraid of.. it is to be received, embraced & treasured because it is an extremely powerful gift from God Himself!

I encourage you seek God about receiving the Baptism of the Holy Spirit with the evidence of speaking in tongues.

If you are currently in a Church Home that does not believe in the Baptism of the Holy Spirit with the evidence of speaking in tongues – RUUUNNNNN!!!! If you do not have a church home, prayerfully ask the Lord to guide you - and He will... I am living proof!!

You Are Now Blessed – in Christ, with every spiritual blessing in heavenly places... go discover what they are!!

Yours in Christ... *Erika D. Newton*

Floetic Ascension of a Lotus

Erika D. Newton

ABOUT THE AUTHOR

Erika D. Newton grew up in the Western Edition of San Francisco, California. As a child of the 80's, Erika unwillingly began to collect experiences that should have never been garnered by a child. Those same experiences pushed and pressed their way into her adulthood, but the story doesn't end there.

Erika has used her past as a launching pad into her beaming present and illustrious future. She is an Author, Floetic Lyricist/Songwriter who is truly inspired by God Himself. She ministers with vision and passion so that others may be lifted up, inspired and encouraged.

With a heart for the youth, she is an active member of NewBirth Church in Pittsburg, CA, where she has served as a teacher for 'Pre-Ignite', a curriculum based Pre-Teen Youth ministry. She is currently working on releasing a Floetic music cd as a tribute to Jesus Christ – exalting His Name & honoring Him using the musical talents He has so graciously given her.

As a testament of God's faithfulness and divine healing, Erika's goal is to allow God to use her to minister His Word in multiple mediums. She looks forward to writing more poetry, short stories and stage plays that will tug at the hearts of those who are lost and teetering precariously on the edge of hopelessness.

Erika currently lives in Northern, CA and has four children and three grandchildren.

Floetic Ascension of a Lotus

www.ingramcontent.com/pod-product-compliance
Lightning Source LLC
LaVergne TN
LVHW011419080426
835512LV00005B/159